Lacewing Days

Lou Davies-James

Lacewing Days

Copyright© by Lou Davies James

All rights reserved. No part of this book may be reproduced in any form, by any means electronic or mechanical, including photocopying, recording or my any information storage and retrieval system without permission in writing from the author.

Printed in the United States of American

ISBN 978-1-387-69029-9

Cover Art:

Grace
LunaSea Altered Art
Lou Davies James
Winterport, Maine 04496

Cover Design by Lou Davies James

Author Photo:
Wallflowers

Forward

And Still

The moon is high
the world is wide
I will clasp joy
against my side.

Though darkness calls
and acts the thief
I will not lose
her in my grief.

I feel the sun
warm on my face
to lend me light,
heart full of grace.

I know it comes,
to sorrow each,
but gladness still
within my reach.

As fragile as breath, tender and swift, life passes. We try with all we are to catch it in our arms, moving through years clasping our joys and sorrows to our breast; the culmination of days we call our own. We rise and fall and rise again blending strength and fragility. How fleeting are the days that slip away. And still....we go on~

Hope is the thing with feathers
that perches in the soul-
and sings the tunes without words-
and never stills at all.

-Emily Dickenson

Dedication

To my father, William W. Davies, who kept tucked in the most sacred places of his soul, the flame of his Welsh ancestry; bardic words kept on the edges of his tongue, forever tended.

I miss you Dad and will always be grateful for the love, history and lore you filled me with.

You always saw me.

My Dad loved this~

I must go down to the seas again
to the lonely sea and the sky,
and all ask is a tall ship
and a star to steer her by;
and the wheel's kick and
the wind's song and the
white sail's shaking,
and a grey mist on the sea's face
and a grey dawn breaking.

from Sea Fever
by John Masefield

Table of Contents

Forward
Dedication
Table of Contents

Catching Bliss	5
Girl-Child Sacred	6
To Be Green	7
A Million Summer Dreams	8
Variations on a Theme	9
Water Bourne	10
Beyond Dust	11
Answerable	12
Salt and Wood-Smoke	13
Nana's Spring	14
Running Backwards	15
In Spring	16
One Morning in March	17
No Seal Untried	18
Mama's Tears	19
Lost at Penmon Point	20
Spinning Light	21
Just Be	22
The Pull of the Moon	23
The Zen of Pebble Dancing	24
Only Some	25
Thinking Out Loud (8,9,17 & 20)	26-30
Okay	31
In Keeping	32
In Haikurra Garden	33
Autumn Endings	34
All for Flight (for Josh)	36
Harmonics	37
Move-In Special	38
Singing the Sacred	39
Turnings and Their Aftermath	40
Water Call	41
Airless	42

Hubble	43
Retirement Squared	44
Your Fall	45
Echoes	46
Grass Whispers	47
Cover My Ears	48
In Between Here and Dreaming	49
Consigned	50
Beach Art	51
In Silver Veins (leaving Colorado)	52
...and welcome	53
Sifting Snow	54
Hum	55
All to Dust	56
Ascension	57
Ghost Writer	58
Ending Grace	59
Innumerable	60
Days at Stony Creek	61
Awash	63
In Pools of Light	64
Courses Run	65
Walking at Waltham	66
Drowning in Autumn	67
Clippings	68
For Whom the Pen Writes	69
Clay and Paper	70
Making Lumpia	72
Mirrors	73
On Task	74
Trill	75
Lacewing Days	76
As Autumn Turns	78
Shift	79
The Felicity of Joy	80
Dreams and Silken Strands	81
A Study in Forgetfulness	82
Train Song	83
Morning Storm	84

How Silently She Sings	85
Kudzu Dreams	86
12 x 36	87
Nuptials	88
Making Soup	89
Of Stones and Flowers	90
One Cup for Turning	91
One To Wish Upon	92
One Rose Blooming	93
Orchard Dreams	94
Riding May	95
Sea Song Rising	96
Sparrow Song	97
The Path of Water	98
The Science of Birds	99
On a Star	100
Cali Rose (for Miss Cali)	101
Beatific Clay (for Erin)	102
A Day for Rain	103
My Last and Only Uncle	104
On Becoming Real	106
Petal Pink (for Mya)	107
Night Whispers	108
Winter Beach	109
In Turning	111
The Ocean	112
About the Author	113
Acknowledgments	115
Index	117

Catching Bliss

Sunlight spills and pools on
my grandmother's patchwork quilt
through the thin, embroidered
curtains in my room.

I step into the day
opening doors and windows
drawing in the morning air
cool off the ocean
feeding cats and kittens on the deck

squeezing juice and sipping as I write
what spills and flows,
feeling it come, letting it go,
lulled by errant phrasing as I stir

dusky berries into batter
fresh cut lemon stinging
winter-weary splits on my thumb,
singing Joni Mitchell

as I wash the spoons and bowls
and smell the muffins rising in the heat.

Sweet days and dreaming,
bliss measured in moments,
fleeting in the light that pours
through my open windows.

Girl-Child Sacred

In the early years the girl is free
connected to the Holy by her breath…

With sunshine-
climbing high in trees to reach the sky,
cradled in branches, listening as she sways,
heart and limbs- mellifluous harmonics ringing…
One with One in One.
With rainbow colors-
streaming from between her tiny breasts,
the heart chakra singing the sacred
in light that moves from pure heart
to open realms of love and back again.

With starburst-
joy swallowed with the cold night air
as mysteries unveil and
Abuela whispers,
though passed away,
love winging from the places
only children see.
Someday…
they will say it is not so,
that life and God reside in just one place,
not spread across the wilds of earth,
not wrapped in innocence,
buoyant on each breath.

Today-
she owns the truth
she won't be told
she needs no proof
no priest describing
God to her.
It erupts instead-the Spirit of the Universe,
pulsing in the Sacred of a girl.

To Be Green

I wish I was the very highest leaf
atop the tallest bough stretched toward the sky.
If I were such I'd throw off every grief-
not be afraid to live, or even die.

I'd undulate with every gentle breeze
that sweeps and swirls around me in its play.
I'd watch it overhead from on my knees
imagining me green, I'd start to sway.

A casting off of every single woe,
solutions that reside beyond my reach-
releasing all of them I'd simply go
with palms outstretched, to nature I'd beseech.

I'd ask the wind to take me as it will
across the wooded fields, beyond the hill.

A Million Summer Dreams

*Beneath the pastoral hum of summer
and the colored blur of Nana's gingham
dress, of his Lily's golden hair,
Billy Jaeger cries in Fenner Park.*

*Beneath the long-ago, dandelion-smudged
knee of his levis, the puckered edges of a scar
that never healed and never will...*

*Beneath the blueberry stained lips
and the marshmallow toasted days,
the smear of flattened delta mud still clings...*

*Beneath the whiff of fried chicken
and the tang of his sweetheart's pink and sassy
lemonade, napalm...*

*Beneath the impish squeals of his grandbabies
as they run and frolic in the gentle August breeze,
the click and jiggle of ammo, the endless trickle
of an age of unwept tears...*

*Beneath the chain-linked, armored walls
erected to the normalcy of days, he aches
to shake the tally screaming through his
head of buddies lost and fallen-
the chink, the crack, is never sealed for long...*

*Beneath the frisbee tossed and whizzing on his left
and the edge of madness squalling through his nights,
Billy watches bubbles on the wind-
fifty eight thousand...
and a million summer dreams.*

Variations on a Theme

Some days pink-
the inner arc of curving shell
held against the light-
translucent glow.

Often brown-
the solid earth beneath my feet
holding crumbled leaves
that once were green.

Seldom red-
depth and hue of velvet roses
scenting midnight air
with whispered breath.

Today blue-
opened high and wide as midday
vaults above the ground-
as far to fall.

Water Bourne

There are many freedoms
I can not afford,
removed from out my grasp
by feeble limb
or circumstance-
breath held inside my chest
for fear of pain.

But on the water
skimming over
surfaces of glass
without restraint
no anchors holding
me to earth as gravity
unleashes me to fly

The kayak brushes
marsh grass as I go
a veil behind of
morning mist where
egrets stalk, a pure
and perfect grace
I call my own

Beyond Dust

The seasons in their constant circle turn,
a counterpoise of life as well as death.
I balance on the wheel as not to burn
in summer, freeze in winter's frigid breath.

I feel time spin unequaled in my blood,
no slowing down for dreams we birth anew.
When I return again to primal mud
all memory I retain will be of you.

For surely mercy shines when love is born,
its seal upon the heart so well received,
engraved deep in the soul, with passion worn,
eternal pledge that only God conceived.

This love with spirit bred, n'er turn to rust
beyond the time these mortal bones are dust.

Answerable

Oh constant Earth
can you tell me please
what need have I
for your sure foundation,
when my soul is
weightless on the breeze
spurning gravity
in its elation.

Tell me star-shine
all I need to know,
answer questions
with your stellar light.
Guide each step and
show me how to go-
clear as morning
though it still is night.

Whisper waves, that
sweep this endless shore,
swallow gull-song
longing flung by choice.
I surrender
here to ocean's roar-
buoyant on the
tremble in your voice.

Salt and Wood Smoke

Don't keep the roses fresh upon my grave,
a vacant shell is all that's there to grieve.
Beloved, feel me beating in your heart,
my spirit lives as long as you believe.

I know you longed to take me in your arms,
to keep me near, to mend with every glance.
But I am still as close as every breath,
remember how we lived the word romance.

I see the tears and shadows in your eyes,
the open shock of truths you disbelieve.
I'll linger here like trembling autumn days
until you let me go, I will not leave.

Come hold my salt and wood smoke in your hands,
I will not try to run or turn away,
but rest upon your palms when night descends,
till light rebinds the fragile ties of day.

Dreams spill again, they shimmer on your cheeks,
upon the stricken canvas of your face,
through parted lips you taste them on your tongue
as fingers sift through memories and lace.

But surely as each passing season turns,
with certainty beyond what men can see,
I will remain, the ring on hand, in heart--
until you find the peace to set me free.

Nana's Spring

Far have slipped the years but I remember
the hours spent when pots and pans would sing.
Snow outside her windows in December
but Nana's kitchen redolent with Spring.

Geraniums still blooming, snow white curtains
settled fresh like snow on stucco walls.
Wisdom graced with love of this I'm certain-
I hear her gentle voice when trouble calls.

Basil and oregano confusing
the pasta in submission on the boil.
Olive oil, garlic cloves infusing
the boule inside the oven, wrapped in foil.

Herbs hung from the rafters near her ceiling,
berries swum in syrup on the shelf.
Tucked in Nana's kitchen, safe the feeling.
I see it all and smile to myself.

Running Backwards

There was a time I knew that I would fly,
if only I'd run fast enough I could,
just like a bird across the open sky.
I'd do the same today, I swear I would!

I'd cast aside this grownup travesty,
remove the woman, keep the little girl,
undo the stretch of bones with alchemy-
I'd give my childhood days another whirl.

So fleet of foot, I'd climb the highest tree
and own again the world beneath my feet,
(no more the loss of limb by slow degree),
sustained on honeysuckle nectar sweet.

There was a time this form was free from pain.
I look behind me now but all's in vain.

In Spring

Day started hot but now the clouds
are lush and flying overhead,
muted shades of grey on grey-
the wind's insistent revelry
to urge them on.

The grass a swell of violets and wild
berries strewn among the green.
That tender ground still welcomes me
and oh that I could just lie down
with you above me, looking down,
to see it all reflected in my eye.

It starts as mist before the rain
so down the hill I go across the lawn
to gather toys and cushions spilled,
the hammock strung between two trees
and tuck them all away before it falls.

I close my eyes and sing the song of trees,
a myriad blend of harmonies-
of pine and fir, red maple leaves,
of ash and elm, of willow's sway and oak.
We sing the dreams of other Springs I've had.

The lilac boughs sway over me as raindrops
dance against my waiting tongue.
The ruby finch, from Adamar, skips
under branches where her seeds are found.

I hear the bus come up the road.
Reluctantly I rise to meet the girls.
Gramma, they cry with smiles bright,
with open arms and hearts to pull me in.

Spring comes...
it always has, it always will
and I to covet each and tuck away
sacred and revered, my inner might.
The sun, a simple candle, to that light.

One Morning

*Beneath the slipping hem of night
morning rustles oak and pear tree petticoats,
unfurling ocean waves-- a distant hush.*

*Today's the day, they seem to say,
the baby comes, and waiting with expectancy
the world holds still and whispers quiet joy.*

*While safe inside his Mama's arms
there is no fear, no want, no rush
for all a man might be or might become.*

*He simply is. His name a magic pressed
against the lips of days, inherent possibility
and risk, this life a slate for him.*

*I listen to the rush of breezes run,
the wind chimes ringing frantically
and still believe*

*that changes come no matter what we do
and even so the earth will hold our names
and speak them low.*

No Seal Untried

seasons spin
another year near gone…
beyond the frosted window pane
night howls…

looking for
the smallest chink
some tiny place
to enter in
and flood this warmth
with cold

but there is none.

no hole that love
has left unfilled
no space where faith
has left the seal untried.

I hold you
like a field of light,
a covering to keep
me safe and whole-

no icy touch
no reaching through
to steal my heat away

your power, only love

and love is all there is.

Mama's Tears

You sent us out
into the yard,
Nan and I,
the screen door
slamming shut-
a summer sound,

armed with loads
of golden ears,
when we were done
their silken strands
left lying everywhere.

Apron tied around
your waist,
you took them from us,
wiping tears away
from reddened eyes-
blaming things
that grew
beneath the ground.

Lost at Penmon Point

Distant calls the evening bell
Faint upon the boson's ear.
Swallowed by the rising wind,
Stars to neither guide nor steer.

Lashing waves against the prow
Threatening to take the ship.
Eyes still strain relentlessly,
Seeking land through swell and dip.

Meaningless, the compass rose,
Direction without bearing.
Reconciling death and sin
With frantic oaths and swearing.

Is it brutal rock on wood
Or the scrap of grief on bone?
Love can rend the darkest night
But it will not lead them home.

Standing watch upon the shore,
Stricken hearts cast out to sea,
Women wait, as women do,
In their weighty agony.

Spinning Light

Why in these narrow confines must we weave
and spin these threads of thought to precious cloth,
releasing breath of angels to create
soft skeins of light that draw as flames to moth.
How in the darkest cell we scratch and spin,
unearthing pain and trembling memory
that shuns the light but in the spill begin
to set the place ablaze so one might see.
The One who travels near, takes silk in hand
and turns it to admire in the glow
the open heart exudes as it expands,
illuminates the path on which we go.

The seeker and the sought, a woven pair,
entwined beyond the weaver and the wear.

Just Be

Low tide water laps and lulls,
a constant hiss and swell.
I enter in, and sluff away
the sorrows of the day
with garments lying damp on
night-drenched sand.

Ebbing cool engulfing skin,
I dive, enveloped
by descending waves-
swallowed whole
spit out again,
tossed upon this
shell-strewn April beach.

Walk instead, along the shore,
one treasure hunter
seeking what may come-
time-worn splint and polished glass
gleaned and gifted by the coursing tide-
drawing signs and wonders as I go,
knowing to the bone they lie within.

So I sit and listen,
sun lands where it will,
and breathe, just breathe...
my rhythms rise and
fall, tied to the sea,
to fill the places tucked
inside the soul,
tossing to the wind
my errant will.

Just be, the sea song
hums against my ear...

just be...just be...just be...

The Pull of the Moon

The circles turn, unceasing,
in my flesh, along each limb,
inside the feral heart-
open and unfettered as the tides

where desire ebbs and flows,
comes and recedes,
lulled or lush-
this mortal ache, the
pulling of the moon.

By night, I wander, searching,
by the sea. The words
I've written sipped and
then consumed, cast and then
unbound I watch them fly.

I feel the earth surrender
to my need, beneath the feet
that anchor me alone-
unmoved yet loosed by
winds that thresh the soul.

On this, as each, I offer
all I am on snow-white sand,
the altar tended here-
a joining, me to earth, to sea,
to sky, to fire- burning sacrifice to love.

I spin and sing those circles
as they go- unyielding turns
of change and endless time,
till heat, dispersed and fractured
glints and gleams, forever
perched and cradled in the stars.

The Zen of Pebble Dancing

I threw a pebble in the sea today
and watched it roll and tumble in the waves.
Control is not my own, it seemed to say-
this is the way a pebble tossed behaves.

Just like a stone I stumble through my days,
am lost above the earth, beneath the sky,
and anxiously confused by pebble ways-
the questions rage within, I wonder why.

But I must catch my breath, as well I might,
enjoy the rolling motion of the tide,
the shush and lull of sea-song in the night
and to the salty water dreams confide.

No need to fight the motion, I am free,
embraced by life with total buoyancy.

Only Some

Some of my laughter
some of my tears
to fill the waiting hours

not nearly all

the deepest part of each
I tuck away, in keeping
for the days still yet to come.

for the moment
it is said, to live one's life
but in the twilight hours
between wakefulness and sleep
the recess of the heart is evident

so much that twines together
in that place, the thens, the nows,
the what may bes tangled and unyielding
a space where logic has no hallowed part,
no place to stand.

It's morning and I go about my way,
tripping over all that must be done.
Some of my laughter, some of my tears,
some of them tightly bound

not nearly all

Thinking out Loud

4.
Where does love live?

Most say the heart-
alive with every
constant beat
cause when it's gone
I know its absence
 in my chest..

or in the blood
through veins that sear
each part of flesh
where circulation
courses, never still.

I feel it
in my belly though
and want to wrap
my arms around
me there
to keep it in.

Or
is it in my hand,
trembling
like a timid bird
forgetting how to fly.

8.

There is always
a crisis.

Sometimes
I hold my breath
in the quiet space between

afraid to just relax
and let things be
for fear the other
shoe will drop

cause drop it will.

Needs to be met,
just not my own
and sure they are...
another catastrophe
averted.

My Mother always said
at such a time
"another one dead
and no water hot."

I have no dead
to lay out yet
so I guess things are okay.

9.

I throw these words
like pennies in a well..
my wishes just as spent,

I watch them fall...
and sparkle in the light
as they submerge.

We make our luck
of that I'm pretty sure.

10.

*I tied my tongue
with my own hands
my heart wrapped
up in bright becoming bows.*

*I dress these pages
up in silken skeins
that catch the light
and urge their swift untying.*

*What treasure here,
my gift to you...
what then within,
a worth beyond all else?*

*The paper strewn
when you are done
and in your hand
inconsequential dust.*

16
it never shuts its mouth
whispering in quiet moments
when she thinks herself alone...

what if...

screaming without mercy-
heard above the din
of every crowd where
refuge is a joke she doesn't get.

you should have...

and hands over her ears
do little good when voices
carry from inside
riding on the blood
inside her veins.

17.
Redolent with garlic and onions
cumin and chili, I simmer in the kitchen-
stirring the watched pot.

Tomatoes diced, oregano
and cayenne, cocoa & coffee,
tenderloin and coriander
mesh and become one

with different beans
a pinch of salt, brown sugar
and dark beer, brewed with
reflection, the anticipation of

sweet and spice. The memory
of each making my mouth water,
my belly growl... as I wait.

20.

Let it age until the cover blows off-
fermentation will do that,
a mix of sweet and sour building
till the vessel swells and seams give way.
I like to turn the valve instead,
to let a little pressure out
to keep the status quo on even ground
and off the ceiling where I keep my sights.
Maybe those are stars instead
it's all perspective anyway,
and not the spattered remnants
of what used to lie within.

Okay

There are crazy-maker days-
when up from down is
too far out of sight
and I can't tell the difference
anymore but just go on....

I remember what I can
that soothes, if I forget,
especially trees
that ask me to let go,
to let it be....just be
alone with where I live
and my own truth

their branches
holding up the sky-
they hold me too,
make sure I see
the beauty of each day
not just the pain.

I listen-
leaf refrains
in familiar voice
that say it is okay
it all will be...
that up or down
it all will be okay..

In Keeping

*I listen well
for every errant breeze
that speaks my name
and calls me home
with your familiar voice*

*I watch
where shadows fall
my dreams in sunlight's spill
or moon's soft glow
I see what is not there
and draw it close*

*breath inhaled
to catch the salty
tinge upon the skin
my fingers ache
to brush,
my lips to taste*

*wrap me up
in what my senses know
though fate deny
let me wander thus–
I will be fine–
love's eidolon
in keeping
at the corner
of my eye.*

In Haikurra Garden

Tremulous

Momiji sways-

Whispered call of freshening wind
strums the temple bells.
Echoes tremble in the flesh,
resonating chimes ring long, ring deep.

O' sweet call to prayer.

Tuning fork resides within,
muscles clench to
keep that thrum alive.

Captured chant
repeat, released

Limbs and soul spread wide-
on gingko wings
high and aloft-
to edges where their
soft sounds fall away.

Autumn Endings

Head into the wind,
sidewalk cracks avoided
on my way to sweeter
dreams and days held
beneath a sky where
oaken castoffs skitter
as they fly.

Beloved take my heart
in autumn days
to gilded fields where
apple branches woo the
little girl who ruled the world
and claimed each day
when I was still a boy.

Fleet of foot and
loose of chains that
bind me where I stand-
a once upon a time
unfettered rose,
though roses fall away
in shadows filigreed
against what light is left
sifting through these
branches yet to climb.

Season's spin
the years turn as they will-
burning leaves and bridges
sting my eyes. Now, as ever,
heart-song set in stone
sealed against what barren
days may come.

I close my eyes again
and breathe you in, to
feast upon the contours
of your face, your endless
summer heart, the heat of you.
I feel my weight
rest easy in your arms,
now and always
sacred and adored
as leaves decay
and autumn endings
scent the air with life.

———————————

All for Flight

For years I was just Mom, my children small.
They looked into my eyes to learn the way.
I kept them close to kiss them should they fall
or wander off, from my protection stray.

I wondered at their gaily spreading wings
and knew the day would come they chose to fly
and in the way of tender growing things
shed their chrysalis, take to the sky.

My sadness held within as they took flight,
they did not see the net I held below.
Marveling that colors are so bright,
I lay in summer fields to watch them go.

We spend these passing days as life demands
but sometimes…they still light upon my hands.

*for Josh

Harmonics

Hum your song
against my skin-
wordless as you
scribe and play

rhythmic waves
against the sand
of my resistance-
the shush and lull
of resonant je t'aime.

Melodies caught
trembling in the throat
convince me for a time
that we are free-
entwined in every

chorused night's design.
Glissando ache
connecting limb and light.
Just shooting stars
in concert overhead
for their refrain.

Move In Special

Three roads leading to the beach,
thirty miles from the city's heart-
construction blighting land and sky
and marsh at every turn,
the constant pulsing race
to get, to have- consume!

No balance struck.

A hundred trees and all they hold
for every gas station,
mini-mart and nail salon,
one thousand for each Wal-Mart Super Store
in this Mecca rich with youth and false success.

The need to own, to grab- collect!

Condo tracts stand ready, set to go-
there's a move-in special-
concrete poured.
More surfaces reflecting back
our brutal Summer sun;
pebbles in a pool whose ripples
splash Antarctica and on.

New SUVs parked row on row,
it's Tuesday, Margarita Night in Jacksonville.
Snow white egret wading deep
in drainage ditches littered with
our refuse as he feeds.

Singing the Sacred

Cayuga Lake's asleep again,
ice-locked at her edges.
Dressed once more
in shreds of white,
organza, wispy curls
across her skin-
beauty lying deeper
than her dreams.

Denise and I would skate
when we were girls,
flying toward each other
till we met and locking hands
would spin in dizzy circles,
laughter pealing bright
in frigid air;

Innocent of life to come
and choices made,
of sorrow bearing arms
against the days
that rush ahead
with thawed intent-
the seasons spinning too.

Will you hold me
in your arms
as winter turns,
as icy stages thin
then melt away?

Singing to the Sacred,
the mocking bird
as Christmas comes-
in the flowering pear
whose leaves are just now
loosening on the bough.

Turnings and Their Aftermath

from troubled thought
I try to turn
and seek instead
the good and gay-

but should and ought
a ceaseless burn
within my head
can only pray

it all goes by
the things we hold
and try to clasp
with fingers tight

they ache to fly
and leave us cold
from out our grasp
resuming flight

no ancient one
with wisdom clear
can ease the mind
or soothe the bone

when all is done
it as I fear
heart undefined
and all alone

Water Call

I walked today toward the sea.
The clouds like eider in a down-filled sky.
No on, save I, to mark my going
between dune and reed
as the sea, siren song calling,
whispered my name again.

Drawn as ever by the lap and lull
of water seeking its high line
I went through heat soaked sand
as the sun climbed toward its own.
Wind over the rise and fall of waves,
spray skipping forward;
 a token kiss brushed on lips.

Drawn forward-
lulled by moving water
till the hiss and foam wrap my feet in cool.
I always close my eyes.

Face tilted sun-wise
as the sea song plays-
familiar calling-
whispered breath against my cheek.
Closer...she says.

Skin heat-bathed shudders
at the foreknowledge of an icy embrace.
The ebb and flow of patience...waiting.

Arms stretched high
as the billowing foam slips-
pooling at my feet like melting cream, I dive.
Swallowed whole by the falling waves.
Love and forgiveness breaking
on the beach of my heart.

Airless

I want to rock like mourning-
gasping hard for breath that will not come,
dragged and drawn to lungs that fight to fail;
silence lost among the piney boughs
that shiver overhead and guard the dark-
a reckless arbor holding out the light

The water beckons, satin on the lake
and promises to wrap me tenderly-
a softening that swirls as edges blur,
cold but not so much as in these veins
where ice would be a welcome friend
to block the things I never wished to see.

The runners on the porch creak back and forth,
a comfort in the battered time-worn chair.
Wood and flesh, a binding of the soul that keeps
me here and will not wash away
or let me take the steps to water's edge
though urgently the violet sunset falls.

Hubble

Far beyond
the realm of Earth
I fly
collecting light,
the birth of stars
and eons past, unfolding
in the mirror of my eye.

Coaxing from those frames
universal timelines-
fourteen billion years and counting

as I sip

galaxies and nebulae
in Ritchey-Chrétien Cassegrain
acts of requisition

digital data
transferred
back to earth
from apertures that widen-
wonder stretched
across the widest field.

Concave and convex
to catch a million miracles
in glass ground to infinitesimal shine-
spherical aberrations corrected.

Defining Galileo's dream
to see more, see farther, see deeper-

buoyant on the breath
of God's own sigh.

Retirement Squared

*A new way of dancing
through the days-
the do-si-do
of keeping off our toes
with no collide.*

*Fresh routines
to set in motion-
choreographed moves
of tune and grace
designed to foster flow.*

*Today you have
no snooze alarms to hit,
just fifteen minutes more
no longer holds-
you get to sleep in every day-
a chance to choose.*

*Still...
I'm awake at six a.m.,
circle left and back again,
to weave among
the patterns of my day
in quarter time.*

Your Fall

I hear you on the
wind and in the rain-
with open mouth I
try to drink you in.
I sip and swallow
hard and try in vain
to find the place I
end and you begin.

You buffet me while
drenching to the bone,
a wet that runs in
rivulets and dreams-
where petals spread
like roses overblown
unraveling what
binds us at the seams.

My Love, you always
were a hurricane
and I unleashed and free
upon your back-
the beauty of your
tempest my refrain,
harmonics sung to
thunder's strident crack.

I never cared for
sunlight's rise and all-
instead just leave me
standing where you fall.

Echoes

My heart is muffled
		in cotton wool
		and so is the sound
		of my voice.

I see what is beautiful
		still, in this life
		and do, as if I
		had a choice.

But all of the grace and joy
		in the world
		is kept just
		a little away.

I nestled it close in this
		hollowed out space
		and willed it and wished
		it to stay.

I know love is kind,
		both gentle and raw
		and rests in the palm
		of my hand.

With all of my wishing,
		and plead as I might,
		it still will not brook
		my command.

Grass Whispers

I left the shore
as the sun rose-
kayak skimming
surfaces of glass
wind through marsh grass
whispers sacred names
against my ear-
I listen well
and tuck them
in the recess
of my pack,
till I am free again-
to mull and turn them over
in my hand.

Cover My Ears

what is this thing that should stay mute.
that burrows round the sturdy root-
that niggles round and tries to hide
where love has come to hearts allied

the voice that does not brush the cheek
but bends the knee in service weak
the creeping doubt in darkest night
where shadows play and quench the light

oh could that I that whisper quell
and end the drone of sorrow's spell
the heart still beats I am not dead-
a whispered truth inside my head

love does not die, but loneliness
rebukes the vows our souls confess
and though my love I can not see
I know he turns his eye to me

I will not hear nor yet believe
that you are gone- I will not grieve!

In Between Here and Dreaming

Between this place of dreaming and awake,
betwixt what might have been and what will be
there lies a place where love need not forsake
the waves inherent knowledge of the sea.

In still warm sand, midnight sky above me,
clouds scud like God's own breath before the moon,
while spirit, free of form, wings outward toward thee
with clarity of sight, as were it noon.

Glow of a thousand moons enjoin us now,
stars of a million skies lend us your light,
song of eternal wind and wave avow
somewhere along the way known souls unite.

Bound with the vales of mist as mornings rise,
you, in the inner circle of my eyes.

Consigned

Tumble me over
the swollen-belly moon,
hang me on
its raw and arching curl.

Sink me under
ocean's teeming currents,
lift me, let me rise
as waves unfurl.

Cradle me, held
in arms of burnished umber,
protected, stone-cleft
sanctuary found.

Christen me pure
with sky, with dark sea water.
Bury me deep
within your sacred ground.

Beach Art

The waves ran high today
For here.
Sibilant surf song raging
Ripe with frenzied foam,
Pounding.
Waves relentlessly
Washing away
My sand scripted poetry-
Just a name.

So…steal what I have written!
Draw it back sea bound
Suck it down and in
Toss it
Windward on dolphins plumed spray.
Mist of life.

Lying on the night damp sand
Fragments of yesterdays
Shells and dreams
Molded to my flesh
A mosaic
Of hips and coquina
Of sand and beach glass.
Eyes closed to the
Wash of sun spilled heat and light.
Lips, tongue lashed
To taste what clings so close.

Breath of life
Salt of my earth
The sea calms
Gently swells
Heaving
Like the rise and fall
Of my life.

In Silver Veins (leaving Colorado)

You weave through every barren plain
that spreads unyielding, beyond sight-
silver veins of iridescent light.
Reflections snake, and coil back,
winding out and splaying through
each ridge of reconciled belief-
molten liquid brilliant in the dust.

I am, you said, the birthplace of your heart,
immersed and swaddled, cradled in your Nile-
the whole and holy shrine of waiting's end
where truth refused to fall against my breast.
Could it be told, I rained enough
to teem and flood each sloping bank,
enough to let me wallow and resume.

One amber gem beneath your surface sank-

once counted,

slightly sullied,

catching breath.

Just before the sun retreats,
fades to dark against earth's acrid edge,
throwing every lingered ray aloft-
at twenty thousand feet I'm stricken dumb.
Boundaries crossed,
life leaves me where you lie,
naiad swooning, caught in your embrace.

I wonder, as you swell and sip the moon,
am I reflected in those sodden depths?

...and welcome

it's grey and blustery –
my favorite kind of day,
the windows open wide
as curtains billow
freshening stagnant air.

I am surrounded-
by ringing notes
in front,
those faerie bells
that rival
childish joy-

cathedral chimes
in the ancient oak
behind the house,
their resonation
thrumming
deeper places-

my cats are in
the windowsills
wishing they were
wild-
for today.

I listen-
to the breath of all,
especially the wind-
who presses
salty kisses
on my brow.

Sifting Snow

I bought a Chinese fan today
at O'Houlihan's on Cayuga Street,
cream colored silk. A hand painted
willow girl, colors muted with age,

kneeling on a long ago scarlet rug...
her face so like my niece, Jiang Shi Ting,
carried in the arms of my two sisters from
the Shaoguan orphanage, bourn away

on an ancient bus, a bone-jarring ride
over washed out roads to Guangzhou.
Grace, Margaret...and Emily, with
rosebud mouth and guarded eyes.

Her fingers poised with gentle grace over strings
pegged and tuned on a dragon's back, notes rising
heavenward through blooming cherry boughs,
scrolls, ink and brushes resting beside her.

Spring at least one snow storm away
on this Central New York morning.
In Shaoguan plum blossoms
stretch and swell in the falling light.

I move the fan in quiet arcs,
kneeling on a moss green braided rug,
the woodstove crackles,
oak acrid, cherry fragrant.

Breath of China falling soft
against my winter-weary cheek-
lost in thought, caught in dreams
where Ithaca meets Guangzhou.

Hum

What eyes have I but these to see what lies
intrinsic, spilled and spattered in the stars,
as galaxies expand with thunderous sighs
on earth below I hum these simple bars
of music shed in harmony, in tune,
my notes ring clear and pure in frigid air.

So pale am I, in radiance the moon
bestows her light on me without a care
as if I am a speck and hardly seen
in grander schemes invisible to time
her beauty reaches still, a silver sheen
while I pretend she hears my human rhyme.

We each a part of each though unaware
and not as we might fear, so solitaire.

All to Dust

What does morning's rise
imply on palest sheets
hung up to dry
beneath the trees
where locust hum?

They flap and rustle
in the winds
that scuttle off
the nearby sea
where shells are shining-

catching sun..

reflecting moon…

crushed…

by endless wave and sand,
flying in the face of both

adhering to my laundry.

Ascension

Yesterday
you came to me-
a winged thing
awash in shine and shadow

flitting bright
on trembling leaves
kiss of summer
brushing
autumn's face.

Lowered eyes
to highest bough-
the sun, forgotten,
golden on my own

You, my breath's
ascension through it all,
the world as tender
shreds of light-
a clutch of feathers
waiting for me there.

Ghost Writer

When I am lying
in that place
where waking thoughts
tease the edge of dreams,
they come.

Ghosts of lives past
not my own
who grab my hand,
spilling themselves
ink-dressed,
on reams
of waiting paper.

Tales to tell
have they who wait
beyond the veil.
A listening
pen empowered heart
all they need
to breathe again.

Light lent
to a dark existence;
to love anew,
to laugh,
to live,
to grieve.

Whose pen
in years to come,
will spill my days upon the page
and give me life
again?

Ending Grace

the need to step outside,
move back from pain-
from stricken shreds of disbelief
choking like my nerves,
impinged and raw

buckets
full of what will never be
sway left then right-
as tightrope wires
slice the barefoot contours
of each step

with crippled gait
I tread this higher ground.
below, what beckons,
rises and recedes-

looming with
unbalance and regret
for things I've done
for those *I failed* to do.

Innumerable

I counted stones today,
tossed in the dawn-still lake,

sips of tea, (jasmine)… and oranges,
sidewalk cracks avoided.

Tallied them with petals tumbling,
apricot and cream, mimosa rain.

Tucking each away,
like numbered days.

How many love-drenched
candles left to burn?

Days at Stony Creek

We were so young…
playing house at your
family's summer camp,
bathing in the river
as the sun rose beyond
the pine-topped ridge.
I filled the copper kettle
with black-eyed susans
gathered from the tilting fields
that lay splayed beneath
the wilting august sun,
setting them on
a worn wooden cask…
my first altar.

You played for me
under a midnight sky,
the firelight brimming
in your eyes as your fingers
found the desired strings,
you, strumming every thread
that tied my love inside.
It wandered free
to fly among the
singing stars.

I was just a girl then…
new and so much younger
than today, dancing
light of heart into the pyre-
I freely offered
every shred
of who I might become-
with total faith.

A hundred years ago
if just a day,
and pain to wash away
a million dreams.
But still, in spite of all,
I see you there
and hear, against the night,
your music play.

Awash

*In every way that love can be
I ask that it wash over me
to fill the little chinks and holes
and mend the cracks where on it rolls*

*to leave me just a bit less dry
so gardens flourish in my eye
with roses sweet not just the thorn
dew drenched to greet the coming morn*

*oh tender vein of heart-skimmed light
fall over me, your mercy bright,
with gentle warmth to tame the cold
and comfort me when I grow old.*

In Pools of Light

Lay me down
in the slanting rays
that fall to the forest floor
'neath the oak,
as her branches sway,
and the sun and the south winds pour.

Smell the earth
as the seasons turn,
Autumn gold gives way to Spring.
Drink ye deep
of my heat and heart
as the wildwoods thrum and sing.

Bind me now
to the earth and sky,
to the air, to the waves and sea,
knowing that
in the binding fast
we are set forever free.

Courses Run

Beneath the weight of winter's hand
new life resides with bated breath,
though frigid wind sweep o'er the land
the seasons turn away from death.

Ice gives way to water's flowing,
rivulets running to the sea,
hours turn with innate knowing,
setting the ice-locked rivers free.

Crocuses, the snow resisting,
as blossoms rise to greet the sun,
light empowers, life insisting,
the turning course of time is run.

Walking at Waltham

These passing days in gladness spend
In company of one called Friend,
No errant fences left to mend-
We till and tend, we till and tend.

O' riotous and lush display
Of Nature in her disarray
Unbinds the soul and feet of clay-
Our fears allay, our fears allay.

On quiet walks the sacred found,
Camaraderie on holy ground-
Simplicity becomes profound
Where peace is found, where peace is found.

Drowning in Autumn

Beneath a veil
of falling leaves
the weight of status quo
more telling than
the season's turn-
a dozen stones
upon my chest
to tend the years.

Forgiveness comes
when Summer
yields her ground-
a willing dive
beneath autumnal seas
of golden filigree;
the acrid tinge
of our decay
my fragrant panacea.

Remembrance stings
like smoke curls
in the wind-
rising through
what fibers I have left,
splayed across
each variegated dream
and swept away.

Clippings

I've cut these pictures
out for years
visions ached for
tucked away-

snapshots of a soul
that walks discordant paths
winding through
desire and despair

tempting me to dream
this lush abandon
just beyond my
lines of sight
as Autumn turns
her golden face away.

Unrequited lust
for what will never be-
a failed fruition
longed for as eternity
in brilliant shades
of red and gold.

What to keep?
What to burn?
Clippings rustle
crumbled to the ground

I watch them fall

dream-leaves spiral
in the breath
of letting go.

For Whom the Pen Writes

Why to this slate, place I, the pen
To leave some lasting trace,
Some semblance of my inner self
That time will not erase?

What is the point, whose eyes will shine
With all my heart once knew?
Is there someone in years to come
Who will see how my spirit flew?

Can I in truth spill on the page
The joy that I once kept,
The purest love, the highest ideals
That through my soul once swept?

How can I feel familiar
To those who are not yet born?
Will they see some truth in me,
A loss this life might mourn?

Is it the beauty of the words
Or the timeless written art
That keeps me scratching out these lines
Until I must depart?

Do I, in honest reconcile,
Imagine they might see?
Or do I become invisible
If I do not write for me?

Clay and Paper

I wonder what will rise
when I am old, what urgent
veins of thought
will rear their heads
to dress the empty pages.

When silver winds
through every hair
and I am stooped
by time, my memory
a cling the most to
sacred days when I was glad-
with beauty, spilled by love,
upon my face.

It does that-
an inner light
I've seen
with my own eyes!

Don't say how sad is that
to worship what is past,
for every breath we take,
hands in the clay,
to shape and mold
our spirits and the truth
of who we are-

the visions we enwrap
around the world,
and every soul we touch
along the way,

the way we love
and breathe and grieve
the way we sing and spill
and much, much more than that.
And so, my Love, unto the last,
through every tear that falls,
it will remain the same for me
seeped into the lines
of papered skin and slate.

Making Lumpia

She can weave
your soul in Celtic knots-
intricate, entwining
here and now
with ages spent-

or send her lilting voice
across the hills
where birds
abandon flight
to hear the song.

She can tend
each flower,
leaf and stem,
mold it with her
knowing touch
to heal each hurt.

But in her hands
rice paper tears,
the roll not tight,
the spice not right,
no Lola in her past
to lead the way
to train her eye,
her fingers-

or her heart.

Mirrors

*you and life
a violet hush-
days whisper skimming
without mar
to surface-still facade*

*me above
you below-
parallelogram
where water
severs left from right*

*twin mirrors squared
sending light
reflected where reflection
holds its breath-
and yet we see*

*dry beneath
or bathed in air
all still the same-
each momentary ripple
simply that*

On Task

Fresh artichokes
at Clancy's Market today-
I sever tops and stems,
snip each pointed leaf,
lemon and garlic mulled
over... considering.

Mundane tasks
surround the sacred-

heart beats...

and beats...

still beats.

Trill

Why do we so rail the dark and tremble
invoking only life, rebuking death
when in truth our souls do light resemble,
are buoyant on the wings of God's own breath.

Does the spirit in the flesh fall silent
and still, to never sing, accept the hush
of song-less ages with the ear not bent
to recognize the pure joy of the thrush.

Little bird, of beauty unassuming
who lends her voice to every waking dawn,
with quivering reverberations ringing,
no more life's chosen marker than its pawn.

Giving death no thought or comprehension,
yielding to the song her own ascension.

Lacewing Days

There are no happy accidents
no matter what the old folks say,
they don't exist.
Everything predestined
in this purpose-driven life.

No bear or deer, no coyote
on the trails today,
but shimmering above me as I go
a cloud of lacewings
in the pure and slanting rays
pouring through the higher stories
where the tree tips sway
carousing with the sky.

One day among them all-
carnal faeries bent on immortality,
alive on dreams of sun and coitus-
thriving and insistent.

Beauty sweeps me up
and still I walk,
needy and relentless,
scanning paths ahead
for silhouettes against the light
that never wait for me.

Scrabbling up each sky-bound trail,
heat through cool
with morning's endless rise-
descend again,
embraced in the hush
of mold growth, decaying limbs-
each step releasing damp and sweet-
pine breath and azalea.

Ten thousand miles and more;
your spirit casting shadows-
falling at the outward edges
of my sight-
illusive on the loamy forest floor.

As Autumn Turns

Last leaves crepitate
in spindly arms,
left alone to wither
on the vine-
a hoarse and hoary rattle-
an ode to summers
spent and those just gone.

They break away
at my approach
a dry stem tour jeté-
death-dance to
all that falls away on
Autumn's failing breath.

Crushed beneath my feet
as I walk on-
all supple flow of sap
through veins curtailed-
once spring green hope
replaced by this…

by this.

Overhead tree branched sway-
the whispered wind a song
that speaks to me-
of years that turn,
of seasons spent
and chance.

They grind to dust
and blow away
not knowing
what lies waiting
past the snow…
beyond the snow.

Shift

I bribe the Muse
with smiles and tears,
chicanery and ache.
She does not budge-

will not inspirit
words that stumble
on the edges of my tongue-
a suffered mute.

Inchoate are
the verses strung-
unordered strands
that ache for light
when flax is all
they'll ever be.

No alchemy
from fingertips-
no straw to gold
nor night black ore
to diamond's crystal gleam.

Just slips and shreds
of errant thought-
the aoristic inkings
of an open soul.

Only ullage-
the frail and faltered
thees and thous
when higher nouns
have filled the page-

the adjectives untried.

The Felicity of Joy

Oh would that I was ten again
the world viewed from my favorite tree.
Across the woods, the fields, the fen,
the ocean there, inviting me.

And I would slither down its trunk
calling all to come along-
on the sun and breezes drunk
dreams and laughter in my song.

Melody through branches sent
lilting toward the waiting shore.
Down the dunes my clear descent
arms outspread as though to soar.

Fervid feet wave-splashed and kissed,
shells and buckets I'd employ.
Oh the things that I have missed-
the felicity of joy.

* for my boys...Anderson, Benjamin and Harrison

Dreams and Silken Strands

My middle child
twenty-five today,
and I alone
to shuck the corn,
moving past
these kitchen walls
to wander on
deserted island sands.

Only me
to wish and
draw you near,
to wonder if you'd leave it
all behind, to strip away
the husk of all you know,
to put away the safe-
exploring joy.

My middle child
twenty-five today,
and I alone
to shuck the corn,
moving past
these errant dreams-
their silken strands
are lying everywhere.

* for Liam

A Study in Forgetfulness

I've made a study of forgetting what I love.
Not the putting away of things outgrown-
just *not remembered*, lost along neglected
paths of things I come across sometimes,
of rank and file needs that fall away…

a trail of silvered moonlight on the sea,
the lure of empty, wind-dashed beaches
thrumming lust that trembles belly deep,
the upward rush of ozoned air, the turn
before the rains can sweep it clean,
the soak-me-to-the skin-drenched romps
in downpours, freeing outpours from
beneath this fragile gossamer I wear,
the spinning, wheeling-free of arms
outstretched to gather every precious drop
before I disappear, absorbed
like summer rain on desert sand...

…and to sing.
I forget to sing, forget I can
or that I could; the notion lost
that music welled within
and ached to fall against the waiting ear.

It's really not so much a letting go.

I've made a study
of forgetting who I am.

Train Song

I'm rocked
and rolled
along the tracks-
canned heat
drying out my lips-
electrifying hair-
a shock to me.

Outside all muted
gray and gray-
the river flowing-
mist along the hills-
trees in contrast
stark and bare-
snow along their branches
stretched and reaching-
winter laden sky.

Cold and empty
waiting for the thaw
that promises to come-

I hope it does.

Morning Storm

Unleash the storm, God's raucous art-
the wild tempest of the heart,
will sluice each seed so gently sown
and strip the leaves from lilies, blown
before its wild symphony
with greens as far as two can see.

Here we stand, again, again
unbound in elemental rain,
clinging close beneath the flood
each torrent singing in the blood
till waves yield on to rivulet
and seems a dream we'll not forget.

How Silently She Sings

I don't want to spill my guts
across another virgin page,
spattered, scarlet
Rorschach blots to glean
evaluation,
examination,
judgment.

I don't want to leak and drain
what little I have left
from shallow pools
of shadowed ache,
from veins of thought
unsung,
unstrung
through fingers
manic wading.

I don't want to turn me
inside out, exposing
sacred altars kept
to harsher sight
more brittle light,
prefer the night-
its silent voice caressing.

I don't want to hear or speak
those thorn-dipped words
much better left unsaid,
unheard,
a silent bird
caught
in the boughs of mourning.

Kudzu Dreams

Dreams fade in the sun--
a hundred miles of
kudzu from the trees
wears the body thin
but wheels still turn

clackity clack
on twisted inroads,
trespass signs ignored.

It's not the motion
that drives me mad
but the striking clock
and the beating heart
echoing through
guarded places.

I find more scratches
in the dark, livid scars
of frantic pace as
mountains of debris
in my backyard
attempt to seal the pass
for one more day.

12 X 36

A triptych print
of winter-barren oaks,
and I in all
my altered states
ache to stand beneath
their arching boughs,
leaf-dressed and filigreed
against an April sky.

Behind the frame
no sun to see
where black and white
sift finer grains of grey;
branches skeletal
and frail cast
shadow on the
ice-encrusted ground.

Trembling fingers
graze across the glass,
frost blooms
beneath their touch.
My step, though soft,
leaves fractures in the snow,
forget-me-nots and roses
in my hair.

Nuptials

These are the days I count with quiet joy,
a tally of the measure I am worth-
an aching back with labor to employ
and fingernails near blackened from the earth,

a sheltered patch of land with dreams to sow
and mark the progress of all growing things,
a cup to sip the seasons as they go,
and recognize the beauty each one brings,

to bathe in streams that tumble on their way
lulled by their sweet and timeless lullabies
and listen for the wisdom of each day,
simplicity that grounds me as it flies.

Far from the stricken pace of city life
Here I reside, the willing bride of life.

Making Soup

I spent the morning making soup,
my son will come today and I
am counting hours till he does-
pouring everything into the pan,
my hopes and dreams with onions
as they brown, redolent with herbs
and memory.

He is too old to sit upon my lap,
for me to tend the wounds
that plague his mind and heart
with kisses small and murmurs low
and arms that keep the darkest night away-
stroking flaxen hair by lantern light.

His nightmares sink much deeper
than his dreams and monster spray
does little to return them to
the twisting, hollow place
from which they rise.

So I'll smile instead and let him in,
love shining out as bright
as love will dare and ladle soup
into his bowl, where garlic, thyme
and lemon slices swirl
amidst the strength I've
steeped and stirred within.

Of Stones and Flowers

You charge me
with the keeping safe
of walls we've
built between-
with magic words
I order them- say stay!

When sure in truth
I'd knock them all
away and see them fall
each stone before
the last all tumbled down
and crumbled fine as dust
about our feet.

I think we'd fill
the spaces left alone
by its demise,
building something
stronger than that wall.

What choices then?

We walk along its length
our shadows cast
and water flowers
nestled in the chinks
between the rocks
that catch the sun.

One Cup for Turning

Draw me water sweet from out the well
when winter storms replenish all we know.
Long before the trees with blossom swell
the ice-bound season gifts the world with snow.

Snow that saturates the thirsting ground
as aquifers imbibe and drink their fill,
unleashed toward the sea where they are bound
when spring unties the thread of winter's chill.

Chill that painted roses on your face
in March now slips away but still the blush
remaining as your fingers shake, unlace
the garments April sheds in such a rush.

Rush toward summer's arms when ours are old
and frigid winds of change are fresh with cold.

One To Wish Upon

At the water's edge,
plans and penance in your hand
through fingers tumble.

Letting go each stone,
thrown like pennies in a well.
Circles gently spread.

Bargain all you are,
rings and shiny copper coins-
a distant dreaming.

What remains behind?
Just a ripple when you dive-
one to wish upon.

One Rose Blooming

I count each year that races on ahead,
Away from visions best abandoned now;
Although relentless hours continue on
I can not turn away, hope disavow.

Please tell me why some blossoms never fade
Though petals swell and wither on the wood,
Time leaving only thorns, the cruelest blades,
That blow away like dust, as dead dreams should.

Resplendent in my mind, their colors gay,
With fragrance, delicate, to tease the nose.
My eyes deceive; will not accept the truth,
The fact that death comes even to the rose.

It seems to me a dark and mortal sin
To starve the bloom we nourish from within.

Orchard Dreams

Fall descends
on frosted morning
fields of corn
rough between their fallen ranks.

Trailing at the edges
goldenrod and purples,
lush growth rusted through
September steals the show
from summer's verdant green.

Dancing breath before me swirls,
held and blown like a 5 year olds.
Into the orchard, Eden's rival.

Beneath whose trees find I, this joy?
Morning cool gives way as rising heat
kisses apple swollen branches with slanting light.
Bees here too, sipping nectar,
scattered drops beneath these ancient trees.

As I, eyes closed,
breathe deep the drunken mix of
heat and cool sweet and rank,
spent days and horded nights.

Bitter sweetly tucked away.
Treasure to admire
When winter's blanket falls.

Riding May

O' May, you stretch of undulating green,
who sweeps across a sea of fervent blue.
We've woven ribbons 'round and in between
each bough and branch in shades of every hue.

Sweet sanctuary days beneath the sun,
heat tempered by the seasons, gently turned.
We give our hopes their head, set free to run,
until July descends and fields are burned.

We ride till fireflies bedeck the night,
elusive need on frail and dainty wings-
to wish, like falling stars, on every light,
caught in the throat while deepened twilight sings.

O' cherished days we clasp against the breast-
this place where fertile dreams may come to rest.

Sea Song Rising

Sing the song
against my ear
of wind and falling waves,
of coming home.

Echo through the heart
each rise and fall,
call to me where dreams
and visions roam.

Swell and press your
soul within my own,
thrumming belly-deep,
your seal engrave.

Ride the tides
that climax and recede-
buoyant on the crest
of every wave.

Seep into my thoughts
with all you are
as shadows stretch
and lengthen on the sand.

Sift through every
breath twilight distills,
to tremble, resting
in my outstretched hand.

Sparrow Song

Little sparrow on the wing untended
free as any little bird could be.
In solitude your days spent as intended.
Is there a lesson in your song for me?

Here in thorny bramble sing the hour,
despite encroaching gloom- the falling night.
Rise undaunted voice from leafy bower
reveling in every sweet delight.

Are you really sure the day will follow
when you with tender wing take to the sky?
Content to be the sparrow not the swallow
in joyful gratitude not question why.

Watch me little bird I'll do it too,
surrendering to life the same as you.

*for Natalie

The Path of Water

With fluidity
water races toward the sea
speed increasing as it goes.
Outside rill and run
there are places currents still-
simple burble over stone.

Time and water over rock
to burnish all as smooth as glass-
a soothing song
and you the melody.

Open hand
releases water,
lets it flow-
will not hold
what can not be contained.

Trickle

Today
time stills
to let me catch
the echo of your voice-
the edges soft, without aggress,
till only love and water dance
trembling and slow.

Solicitous-
the river waits.

The Science of Birds

Kept beyond the wave line,
breath-caught...
Pelicans and the science
of birds in flight
instilled in four year olds.
Yet inside where I breathe
it's only me-
aching to dive;
to drown the want
in icy thrashing waves,
to stem the tide,
to cool the heat
that roils and spills-
belly dark and deep.

Pounding surf
vibrates through the sand,
echoing bone-sung
rifts and rills
in and out of tune...
the lull and hum of days
when I was one
with every grain of sand,
with air and sea.
I never held myself
apart from life,
from all it offered,
shining, in its hand.

But here they come again
with treasure rare,
feathers found that
fell to earth from flight,
broken shells and wave-kissed glass
tossed and tumbled,
offered back to land.
The olive sea shrugs off
her lacy dress-
with little ones in tow,
I head for home.

On a Star

Require not this supplicant to fall
unhindered as the stars from out the blue,
the one on which we wish for love and all
the hopes that rise within the soul of you.

That fall would leave bright heaven's face askew-
for surely on its countenance belong
each solitary speck we keep in lieu
of needs that shined within us all along.

How is it such desire can be wrong,
to seek illumination, clasp it tight-
one tiny star discovered in the throng
held cupped within the hand to lend us light.

We soar and sweep, we fall, we rise up high
and once in a blue moon our bonds defy.

Cali Rose

the baby's eyes
light up the room
and we are held
by every tiny shine

she entertains

in sing song babble
twinkle, twinkle
melodies arise
if not the words

rocking tight
from foot to foot
arms above her head
in pure abandon

today she moves
for all shes's worth
this moment holding
all that needs to be

* for Cali

Beatific Clay

Precious child nestled in my arms
I hold these moments sacred as you sleep
against my heart and free from every harm
as love embraces us both wide and deep.

Were it fair I'd keep you here with me
at breast and let life go its errant way.
But there are joys and sorrows you will see
to shape and mold you, artist's tender clay.

My sweet beatific own I'll do my part
to nurture vessel and the soul within,
to recognize potential of the heart,
and know denying love the only sin.

My wish for you, a spirit unconfined
and strength to know the peace of your own mind

*for Erin

A Day for Rain

Two old women came to me
as I sat beside the sea.
Smiling faces introduced.
in a heartbeat they seduced.
With genteel ways they said hello.
I smiled back, as those things go.

"I'm Zabella, this is Rain
we've come to walk the beach again."

Belongings handed safe to me
they set off walking toward the sea.
Rain as fragile as a breath
walking arm in arm with death.
Fine white hair in disarray,
age soft eyes took in the day.

Zabella gently took her hand
and led her down the wind-swept strand.
Leaning close like young girls will,
with voices soft as secrets spill.
Taking in the days sweet graces
glorious smiles on their faces

Wise with all their lessons learned,
after a distance they both turned.
With feeble steps returned to me,
to where I sat beside the sea.
Forgetting illness, though in pain,
the time a blessing.

A day for Rain.

My Last and Only Uncle

My last uncle,
sick for many years
with Parkinson's and age
had a stroke today,
eighty-two and falling.
The bathroom floor rising
up with manic speed
where up and downside
edges blur and merge.

Reese, the second youngest
son of ten, the only sibling
Mom has left, the rest
across the years
have passed away-
and she alone to tell the tales
of bygone days
when Mama threw the rocks
at Will to chase him
down the hill and off to school.

Or when she took the ax
to outhouse walls
and damn near
tore the whole thing down
to roust that god forsaken
snake that dared to scurry-
sanctuary found.

I remember too…
mint chocolate chip ice cream
dished out to Nan and I,
vanilla fading into the distant past-
exotic and so new at eight and nine;
the dares we made to tag
that scary, metal frog that grinned

beyond their neighbor's split rail fence.
Tin Easter beach buckets,
Lamb Chop puppets,
Frye boots and fried chicken
as the days sped by,
slipping from our hands,
so soon…too soon.

He e-mailed me
some days ago,
suggesting things
to take my pain away-
spoke of how the hours
fell as well as he,
on occasion when dizzy
set his world askew
and left him lost
unbalanced and afraid.

"The point of no return
must surface soon," he said.

It came today.

———————————

On Becoming Real

How real am I? I breathe the words again,
once held to keep your childhood faith alive
and every demon safely tucked away-
companion bright, invincible and new.

Like bunnies, velveteen, loved into life-
it's only broken hearts that magic mends,
when seen through aching need and threadbare dreams,
those places where the fur is gone, unseen.

My azure ribbon dull as rain-washed sky
lies gently, frayed and tattered, on my chest.
One button eye to see what change may come-
the other lost on cluttered, unkempt shelves.

Like dust motes in the slanting attic light
remembrance sifts and settles on my brow,
the silence deep and still as waiting falls,
collecting in the corners of my eye.

The skin horse waxes spiritual again.
It is, he says, the only way there is.
A flaying of the heart, an opening,
to every welcomed joy and mislaid tear.

How real am I? I breathe the words again,
and watch the leaves turned golden tumble down
while deep within my stuffing snowflakes fall.
I shiver to the bone - await the thaw.

Petal Pink

She broke my night, like morning,
dawn blooming at horizon's edge-
and I fell ...
harder than I ever had, deeper
and impossibly in love.
Soul thrown wide
to drink her new life in.
Promises unfolding
with each breath-
blush of innocence all petal pink.

These last two years
have streaked my hair with grey
and curved my back-
life's trials flying furious and fast,
but she is joy.

I marvel at her
brilliance and allure,
she wraps me with each word
and baby song.
She teaches me
to see the world anew-
possible and pure,
with everything before me,
not behind,
still welcoming.

for Mya

Night Whispers

Sun-drenched sand still hot
in layers down beneath
the cool as twilight falls.
Dig my toes in deep
to know it lingers there-
reassurance of all things
that pass away.

Pillow for my head,
these dunes that swell and dip-
reflection of the
wave-embellished tides.
Ancient sea-crushed
grains sift over me-
a whisper of the truths
alive within.

Buried-
like my feet
beneath the sand.
Soaring-
like the stars
strung overhead;
clear and sacred
pinned upon the surface
of my dreams.

Shhh...she says
and bathes me
in her light;
the Moon
whose secrets mingle
with my own.

Winter Beach

I walked
a winter beach today
though august heat prevails.
Grey sky reflected
on a steely sea.

Mine
the first steps to mark
this water bound path,
thru dunes frosted with
wind sifted sand,
heaped at the edges.
While I slide
toward the sea.

The tide out.

Breakers falling where
only crushed shells tumble,
remnants of yesterdays
wave tossed treasure
missed those years ago
by questing eyes.

A castle.

Sanctuary
beyond the high tide line.
Deserted by occupants
called home to other realms.
I the only princess
to roam its hallowed halls,
along battlements
once unbreachable;
Crumbling now
on this wind swept strand.

No pirates
to rape and plunder,
to carry me off to foreign shores.
No adventure.
Just the rakish call of gulls
resentful of my intrusion.

On this
Winter beach.

In Turning

I know you cringe when I say crone
but lately she is singing in my veins-
an ululating song of loss,
my notes subdued beneath her melody.

I was much younger than I am-
lived days I spent my time in flagrant joy
voice arcing angels in my head
the ache of love songs singing in my blood.

But only now a whisper kept
cupped in the quiet spaces of my soul-
I hear her as I fall asleep
alluding to a maiden moist and free.

I call her out, inviting her
to wash through every hidden place-
erasure of disjointed pain,
the grace I used to hold no longer me.

There is no sorrow in her eyes
she will not come but turns her face away
and in her place the wise one sits-
my name a wordless song upon her lips.

The Ocean Is Myself-1974

The ocean is myself,
a twin to me.
My emotions crashing to the shore,
endlessly,
without an answer.
The waves of my existence,
in an eternal pattern,
fall to their destined places.
And I,
never coming undone
Or losing the constant rhythm,
Go on calmly,
As my world revolves~

In both my poetry and altered art my most common themes are love, in all its forms, nature and the sea, my power place. I grew up very near the ocean and spent many years both as a child and an adult close to the rise and fall of waves and tides, gull caw and siren song. I wrote the above poem almost forty four years ago and I love the ocean still.

And to each of you...

May you live every day of your life.
                -Jonathan Swift

About the Author

Poet and Altered Artist Lou Davies James has been writing for over four decades. As a child she developed a love for the melodic nature of words at her Mother's knee. She is known for touching the reader's emotional core with her tender, lyrical poetry; though it has been said that there are thorns among the roses and care should be taken of the reader's heart. Lou lives in Winterport, Maine with her husband and a slew of elder kitties.

Lacewing Days is her second full length volume of poetry.

Previous works-

Adrift In the Holy, Drawn as Ever and Internal Insomnia

My thanks to all who walk this life with me..
You mean more to me than I can express,
even at my most flowery
I love you~

Index

12 x 36
A Million Summer Dreams
A Study in Forgetfulness
Airless
All for Flight
All to Dust
...and welcome
Answerable
As Autumn Turns
Ascension
Autumn Endings
Awash
Beach Art
Beatific Clay
Beyond Dust
Cali Rose
Catching Bliss
Clay and Paper
Clippings
Consigned
Courses Run
Cover My Ears
Days @ Stony Creek
Days Behind
Making Lumpia
Making Soup
Mama's Tears
Mirrors
Morning Storm
Move-In Special
My Last Uncle
Nana's Spring
No Seal Untried
Nuptials
Of Stones and Flowers
Okay
On a Star
On Becoming Real
On Task
One Cup for Turning
One Morning in March
One Rose Blooming
One to Wish Upon

Dreams and Silken Strands
Drowning in Autumn
Echoes
Felicity of Joy
For Whom the Pen Writes
Ghost Writers
Girl-Child Sacred
Grass Whispers
Harmonics
How Silently She Sings
Hubble
Hum
In Autumn
In Between Here
In Haikurra Garden
In Keeping
In Pools of Light
In Silver Veins
In Spring
Innumerable
Just Be
Kudzu Dreams
Lacewing Days
Lost at Penmon Point
Sea Song Rising
Shift
Sifting Snow
Singing to the Sacred
Sparrow Song
Spinning Light
The Ocean
The Path of Water
The Pull of the Moon
The Science of Birds
The Zen of Pebble Dancing
Thinking Out Loud
To Be Green
Trill
Turnings
Turnings and Their
Variations on a Theme
Walking at Waltham
Water Bourne

Only Some
Orchard Dreams
Petal Pink
Retirement Squared
Riding May
Running Backwards
Salt and Wood-Smoke
Train Song